The Box

Architectural Solutions with Containers

The Box

Sibylle Kramer

Architectural Solutions with Containers

BRAUN

CONTENTS

PREFACE

The esthetics of the container is very special. The uniform, brightly colored boxes stacked up on container ships, crossing the oceans and transporting freight to ports of destination, are a familiar sight. But divorced from their original purpose the boxes can do much more, operating as a temporary building ersatz, a rough installation, or an element of modern architecture.

The container story began in 1956 when the first 20-foot-long standard container, the so-called TEU (Twenty-foot Equivalent Unit) conquered the seas. Malcolm McLean, the American freight forwarder, was the inventor. The practical boxes expedited transportation routes and the shunting of goods, permanently altering world trade by the 1970s. The efficiency of offloading freight with containers and loading bridges is eighty times greater in comparison to the pre-container era. Today the great container ships transport more than 18,000 containers to their ports of destination.

Now architecture has discovered the pre-fabricated modules. Today they are used as temporary buildings, as raw implants in a building envelope, or are sent on tour as installations or event projection surfaces. Containers are used for different purposes in architecture. They are deployed as the used, original ocean going container with all the scars of their journeys, and just as well as a new product that can be individually refurbished and equipped. The manufacturers of containers offer package solutions with wall, ceiling and floor superstructures, which conform to prevailing building regulations, like thermal insulation, or high-quality façades which can be custom fitted. The ocean going containers have emerged as original items with their own esthetics. Their characteristic appearance as (transportation) box is a symbol for the journey. The identity granting design is often seen in airport facilities, cruise ship terminals or railroad stations, as the projects Barneveld Noord Railway Station by NL Architects in Holland or the Cruise Ship Terminal by Hombre de Piedra + Buró4 Architects in Seville have shown.

Stacked, strung out in a row, with facings or cut open, the container is an extremely flexible and mutable building with varying functions and design. In crisis regions their quick availability makes them ready assistants as emergency shelters.

The economical standard version of the container permits interim solutions, like that in 1989, when the Wall fell in the former German Democratic Republic and for years property rights were not clear. On a temporary basis automobile dealerships and retail outfits occupied elaborately designed containers.

20 and 40-foot-long containers, 8-feet-wide, and either 8 or 9-feet-high, are primarily used in modern architecture. The original ocean going containers in bright colors and with all the scars of their past are available as elements of stark contrast implanted in purist design concepts, like group8 did for the Cargo project in Geneva. Then again they have surfaced with organic cut-outs and fantastically designed walls as inspiring kindergarten boxes, or zipped open and cut up as a cool bar in a beach club. They can also be seen with completely glazed gable ends, as tastefully designed and fully operational high-quality domiciles with a panorama view. This book shows 45 exceptional examples of redesigned container projects. Their astonishing variety reflects the flexibility of the standardized and combinable container. The Box will never be the same.

Architects: LOT-EK (Ada Tolla & Giuseppe Lignano)
Location: Madison Avenue, New York, USA
Number of containers used: 6
Gross floor area: 720 sqm
Completion: 2011
Type of use: education, art studio

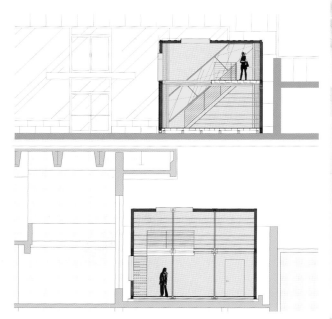

THE WHITNEY STUDIO
NEW YORK, USA

LOT-EK was commissioned to design an art studio space for the Whitney Museum of American Art. The Whitney Studio is located in the Sculpture Court of the Whitney Museum's Marcel Breuer building on Madison Avenue. The Studio houses activities for the Whitney Museum's education program, including art-making classes for adults, teens and families, informal lectures and special exhibits. The building employs six steel shipping containers stacked on two levels to form a monolithic cube, designed to fit the Whitney's open moat on the south side of the entry bridge. Inside, the studio offers a white, double height space for the production and display of art work.

It is estimated that between 2,000 & 10,000 containers
a year fall off ships and are lost at sea.

CRUISE SHIP TERMINAL
SEVILLE, SPAIN

The new Cruise Ship Terminal in the port of Seville was built with re-used shipping containers in 45 days (30 days in work-shop and 15 on-site). It is now a flexible multipurpose space. Between cruise arrivals, it is rented as an exhibition pavilion, a showroom or even as a concert space. The composition is simple and sustainable, in harmony with its urban environment. The open space required is obtained in spite of the limited width of the container. Double-height spaces increase the space inside. Windows let in air to ventilate the inside spaces and special white painting avoids excessive warming. The industrial nature of the containers is evident.

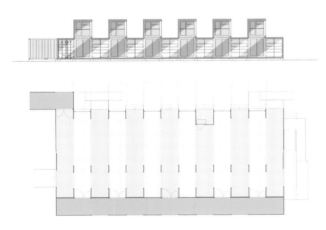

Architects: Hombre de Piedra + Buró4 Architects
Location: Muelle de las delicias, Seville, Spain
Number of containers used: 23
Gross floor area: 508 sqm
Completion: 2013
Client: Seville's Port Authority
Type of use: cruise ship terminal and exhibition center

Around 1.5 million seafarers are employed by the global shipping industry.

Architects: AnL Studio (Minsoo Lee + Keehyun Ahn)
Location: Song-do new city, Incheon, South Korea
Number of containers used: 5
Gross floor area: 91 sqm
Completion: 2010
Client: Incheon City
Type of use: public observatory

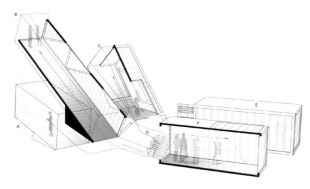

OCEANSCOPE
INCHEON, SOUTH KOREA

Oceanscope consists of 5 recycled containers, which provide an observatory deck (3 containers) as well as a temporary exhibition space (2 containers). AnL Studio envisioned an architectural and sculptural landmark embodying various features and functions, ranging from architecturally framing / capturing the view and esthetics associated with the site and the vision of Incheon City, which is flying. In order to overcome the limitation of a building site where ground level is too low to view a beautiful sunset, the containers can be tilted at various angles (10' 30' 50'), allowing users to climb the stairs at different times and enjoy the various views of the ocean, New Incheon Bridge and the sunset.

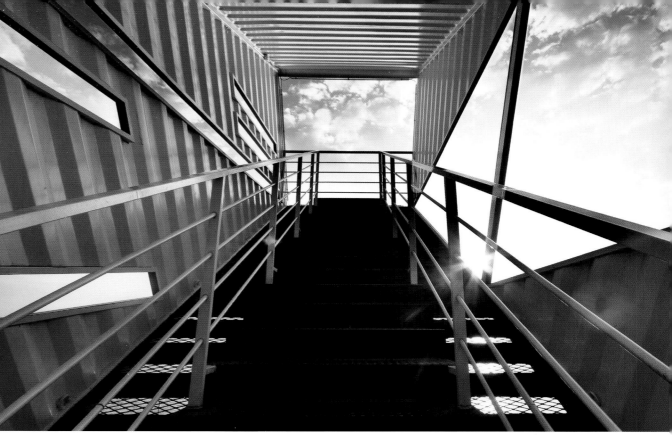

There are approximately 55,000 merchant ships
carrying containers around the world.

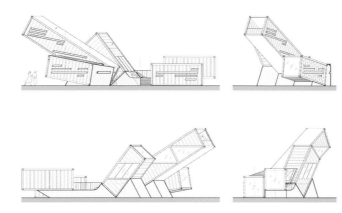

SKY IS THE LIMIT
YANGYANG, SOUTH KOREA

"Sky is the limit" is a domestic space sample, 20 meters above the ground. A tea room projected in a state of weightlessness over the troubled horizon. The building structure is nothing more than a fragile skeleton. Its thin arachnoid structure creates a vertical void. The bicephalous head of this fleshless body is composed of two entities. Two captive voids of similar dimensions provide two opposing experiences.

Architects: Didier Faustino
Location: Yangyang, South Korea
Number of containers used: 2
Gross floor area: 50 sqm
Completion: 2008
Client: Eulji Foundation
Type of use: DMZ tea house

Architects: James & Mau
Location: El Portón de Tarifa, Cadiz, Spain
Number of containers used: 3
Gross floor area: 300 sqm
Completion: 2013
Type of use: residential

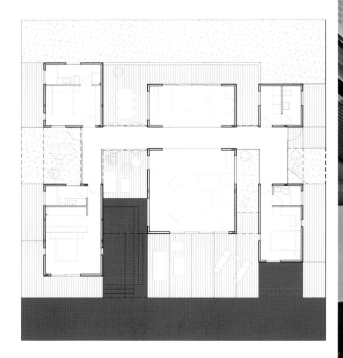

TARIFA HOUSE
CADIZ, SPAIN

The terrain is located on a slope looking at the valley that dominates the Straits of the Gibraltar. The idea was to shrink a "pueblo" on 300 square meters and turn it into a contemporary "cortijo". The first characteristic element of a "cortijo" or "pueblo" would be the wall that defines it. The plan resulted in a series of volumes, just like buildings or pavilions with different functions, which form a "pueblo" or "cortijo". The same mesh used for the pergola dresses the volumes, creating continuity between the false enclosure and the volumes. Furthermore, a variety of empty spaces were created, both inside and outside, which permits one to walk in the house through the multitude of paths, just like in a "pueblo".

A new container in 1970 cost $5,000, while today,
many models are available for only $900.

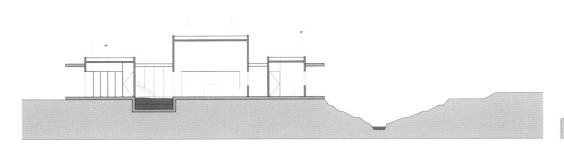

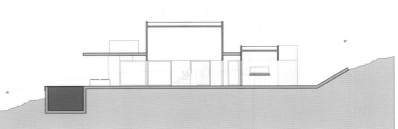

Architect: Sebastián Irarrázaval Delpiano
Location: Los Trapenses, Lo Barnechea, Chile
Number of containers used: 12
Gross floor area: 350 sqm
Completion: 2012
Client: Ricardo Bezanilla
Type of use: residential

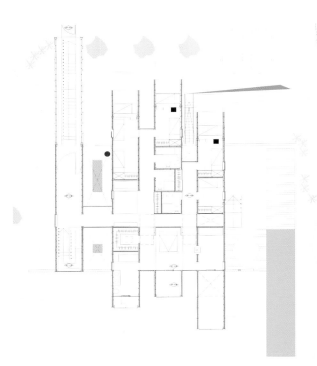

CASA ORUGA
LO BARNECHEA, CHILE

This prefabricated house for an art collector and his family was built in the outskirts of Santiago in a new suburban residential area. In order to reduce construction time and costs, second-hand shipping containers were used: five 40-foot standard containers, six 20-foot standard containers and one 40-foot open top container for the swimming pool. The main purposes of the house were two: the first was to integrate it with this part of the city, where the presence of the Andes Mountain is extremely strong both visually and tectonically. The second was to enhance the air circulation through the house in order to avoid mechanical cooling.

The curb weight of a standard container is 2,300 kilograms for a
20-foot container and 3,900 kilograms for a 40-foot container.

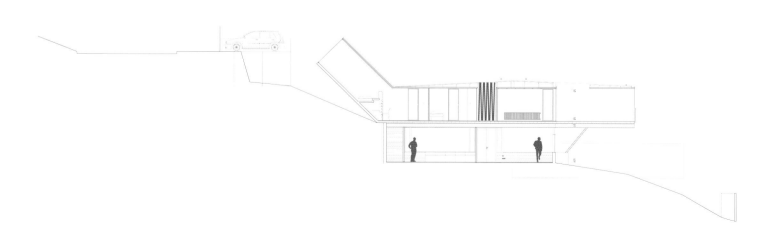

Until recently, a surplus of Chinese overseas containers have been rusting away in the port of Antwerp. "Sleeping Around" gives them a second life and converts these containers into mobile hotel rooms. Since authenticity, comfort, adventure, design and the unexpected are the experiences we all seek, "Sleeping Around" offers a ready-made answer: a compact yet luxurious hotel room, equipped with all the mod cons: a comfortable bed, high-quality sanitary facilities with rain shower, iPod docking station and air conditioning — all put together in a 20-foot recycled sea container. Each cluster of hotel room containers also includes a breakfast / lounge container and a sauna.

SLEEPING AROUND
ALL OVER THE WORLD

Designers: Sleeping Around
Other creatives involved: Didier Opdebeek and Geoffrey Stampaert
Number of containers used: 7
Gross floor area: 20 foot per container
Completion: 2012
Type of use: pop-up hotel

Shipping is cheap. So cheap that, rather than fillet its own fish, it is cheaper for Scotland to send its cod 10,000 miles to China to be filleted and returned to Scotland.

The A'DOCKS campus residence is a significant element of the extensive re-qualification project of the docks neighborhood launched by the city of Le Havre. Located at the end of the Vauban Docks perimeter, the residence, by its nature and architectural conception, creates a link with the surrounding harbor landscape. In order to observe the building code, the architectural approach was to create an independent primary structure to support the containers. This choice lends a great level of freedom to the composition, by playing with volumes and avoiding a simple stacking mode, which would have referred to the traditional function of a container in a linear way. The trick was to play with the different positions of the containers, providing transparency and lightness to the building, and enriching the indoor and outdoor spaces.

CITE A'DOCKS
LE HAVRE, FRANCE

Architect: Alberto Cattani et Charlotte Cattani architectes
Other creatives involved: AR-C, Inex, GTM Bâtiment, Newden design
Location: Le Havre, France
Number of containers used: 110
Gross floor area: 24 sqm each apartment
Completion: 2010
Client: CROUS de Haute Normandie
Type of use: student residence

Sending a container from Shanghai to Le Havre (France) emits fewer greenhouse gases than the truck that takes the container on to Lyon.

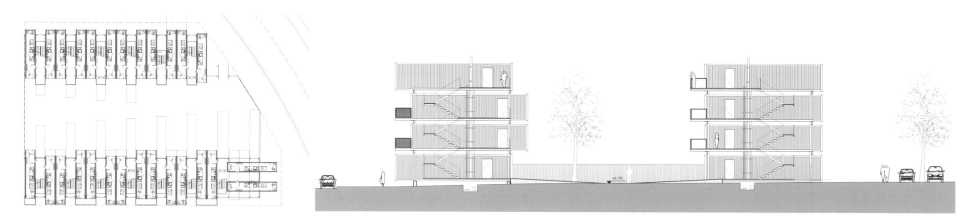

FOLDING RED
BEIJING, CHINA

The "Red" container Art Commercial modular buildings are located under the Oriental Pearl, on the east bank of the Huangpu River. The facility has great flexibility, functioning as an office, brand experience, high-end catering as well as fulfilling other needs. The project aim is to become an important part of the recreation revetment system of the Huangpu River. The design goal was to use, "a container, which is far more than just a container." The red corrugated sheet is the dividing line between the public and a more private area. People enjoy the events and discussions in the open space, while others chat or communicate in the more personal corners.

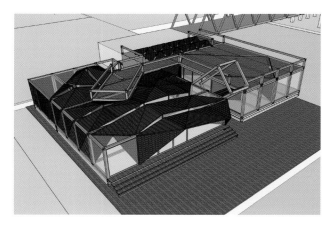

Architects: Beijing Jikerzhicheng Product Design Consulting
Design director: Keli Mo
Designers: Chongxiao Liu, Shixun Feng
Location: Beijing, China
Number of containers used: 4
Completion: 2013
Type of use: exhibition

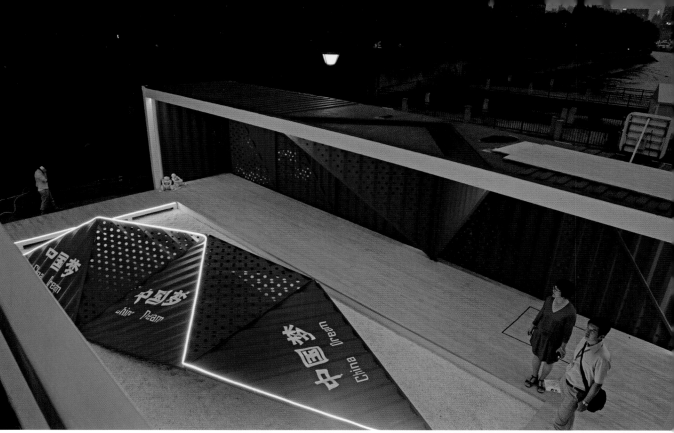

Malcolm McLean and Keith Tantlinger developed the first container specification in 1956. It was an 8-foot-wide by 8-foot-tall by various 10-foot lengths box made of 2mm thick corrugated steel.

HILFIGER DENIM
BERLIN, GERMANY

Similar to the premiere in summer 2010, the maximum visibility from the outside is again most important. This is achieved by covering the container wall with motifs of the current print campaign. In addition, Hilfiger's container booth opens up to the Denim Base of the main Bread & Butter exhibition hall with an open deck complemented by a container pool with glass walls.

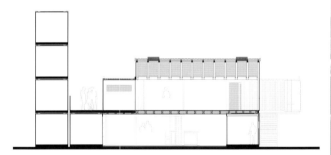

Architects: Artdepartment Berlin (Dipl.-Ing. Peter Weber)
Other creatives involved: Jonas Greubel and David O'Connell
Location: Bread & Butter, Berlin, Germany
Number of containers used: 29
Gross floor area: 346 sqm
Completion: 2011
Client: Tommy Hilfiger Europe BV, Amsterdam
Type of use: exhibition fair stand

Every container has its own unique unit number to identify its owner.

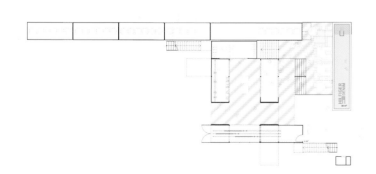

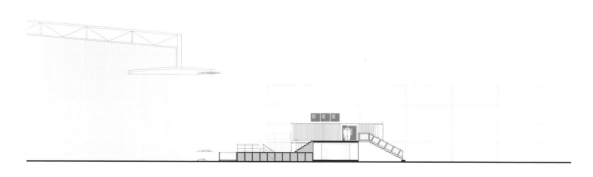

TONY'S FARM
SHANGHAI, CHINA

Tony's Farm is meant to be more than just a place for growing and processing vegetables. The vision of the project is to promote a more natural lifestyle by exposing consumers to the processes of organic agriculture. Throughout the project the immediate spatial relationship between the building and the environment is meant to create a virtual dialogue between the industrial aspects of food production and the surrounding farmland. In order to cope with the high aspirations of the client regarding the protection of the environment, several strategies have been used to reduce the energy consumption of the building and building materials.

Architect: Playze China
Location: Pudong New District, Shanghai, China
Number of containers used: 78
Gross floor area: 1,060 sqm
Completion: 2011
Client: Tony's Farm
Type of use: reception, offices and meeting rooms
combined with an existing production warehouse

In 2009, the 15 biggest ships in the world gave off the same amount of greenhouse gas as 760 million cars. Compared to trucks and planes however, shipping is still the greenest form of transport.

ProRail, responsible for the railway network in the Netherlands, together with the "spoorbouwmeester Koen van Velsen" (the national supervisor for railway architecture) started a campaign to make waiting more comfortable: "Prettig Wachten". Within this program an intervention had to be planned for the train station in Barneveld Noord. Since it was supposed to be a temporary structure, the station is built with shipping containers. The containers both contain and form space. Together they form an ambiguous but strong sign. Minimum effort, maximum output.

BARNEVELD NOORD RAILWAY STATION
THE NETHERLANDS

Architects: NL Architects
Location: Barneveld, The Netherlands
Number of containers used: 4
Gross floor area: 80 sqm
Completion: 2013
Client: ProRail
Type of use: train station

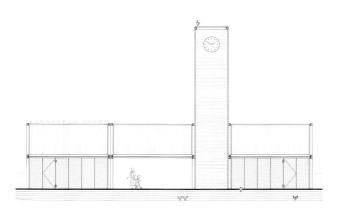

Containers are the strongest mobile or stationary structure in the world, built to withstand typhoons, tornados, hurricanes and even earthquakes.

CARGO
GENEVA, SWITZERLAND

The Cargo project involves the renovation of a former industrial hall converted into group8's offices. A bright space containing a hidden treasure: recycled shipping containers. Following Marcel Duchamp's idea of ready made, these monumental objects acquire a new function, embodying a collective form or a situation of the architects' work: model workshop, cafeteria, sanitation. The other half of the scheme is in opposition to the containers' structured zone: a white and luminous open space which generates a strong synergy of work and gives shape to a neutral environment, favorable to creativity.

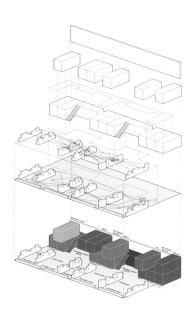

Architects: group8
Location: Châtelaine, Geneva, Switzerland
Number of containers used: 16
Gross floor area: 820 sqm
Completion: 2010
Client: Coopérative Verntissa
Type of use: work space

In 1956, loose cargo cost $5.86 per ton to load. Using an ISO shipping container, the cost was reduced to only 16 cents per ton.

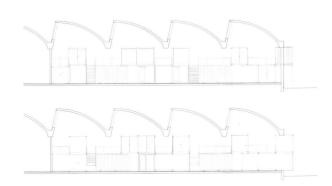

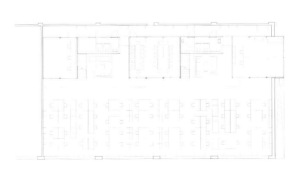

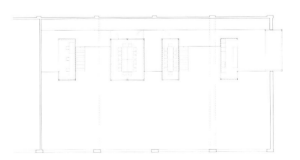

The showroom of the Decameron furniture store is located on a rented site in the furniture district in São Paulo. To make the quick and economical construction viable, the project assumed a light placement on the lot, basically done with industrial elements, which could easily be assembled. The space was constructed with maritime transport containers and a specifically designed structure. Two stories of containers form tunnels where products are displayed side by side. When both doors are simultaneously opened, the whole store becomes integrated with its urban context. During rush hours, by opening only the back doors, the store enjoys the quiet of the inner garden.

DECAMERON
SÃO PAULO, BRAZIL

Architects: Studio mk27 – Marcio Kogan + Mariana Simas
Location: Alameda Gabriel Monteiro da Silva, São Paulo, Brazil
Number of containers used: 6
Gross floor area: 250 sqm
Completion: 2011
Client: Decameron
Type of use: showroom

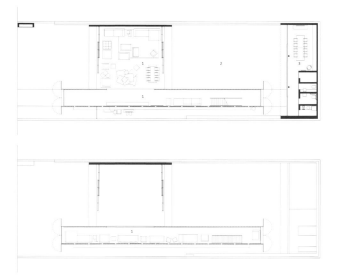

A standard container is 8' 6" high. In addition for the majority
of container types there is the "High-Cube" (HC, also known as HQ,
for "High-Quantity"). These containers are 9' 6".

Architects: FIVE AM
Location: Walle 109b, Kortrijk, Belgium
Number of containers used: 13
Gross floor area: 4,000 sqm
Completion: 2012
Client: Drukta & Formail
Type of use: industrial and offices

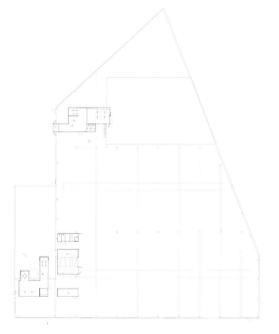

CONTAINER OFFICES
KORTRIJK, BELGIUM

When the going gets tough, seemingly impossible challenges can actually lead to surprising results. The printing firm Drukta and mailing company Formail approached with a limited budget, but with lots of ideas. Their openness of mind was the foundation for these offices, installed in used shipping containers. One of the main requirements was to stimulate interaction between the offices and the work floor, which also had to be experienced by visiting clients and suppliers. Encapsulating the containers in the existing building results in a perfect interaction and creates a unique experience for each visitor.

The shipping container floors are made of planking or plywood,
which is very strong and resilient, does not dent,
and may be easily replaced during repairs.

Japan is the country which importing most of building material. The architectural market price is far above the international market because of expensive Japanese labor costs. The only way to solve this problem is to import finished buildings. Bayside Marina Hotel is making use of shipping containers in order to transport cottage type guest rooms in. As long as the housing can be transported in containers, transportation cost can be kept to a minimum. Cost reductions and shorter construction times were realized by factory assembly in Thailand and transporting the units to container ships to Japan.

BAYSIDE MARINA HOTEL
YOKOHAMA, JAPAN

Architects: Yasutaka Yoshimura Architects
Location: Yokohama, Kanagawa Prefecture, Japan
Number of containers used: 55
Gross floor area: 1,720 sqm
Completion: 2009
Client: Bayside Marina Hotel Yokohama
Type of use: hotel

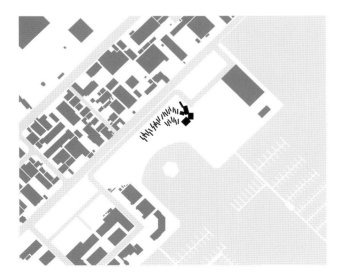

"The cargo containers, with a life span of about 20 years when used for their original purpose, have an "infinite life span" when stationary and properly maintained." – Adam Kalkin, American architect

Architect: GRAFT – Gesellschaft von Architekten mbH
Other creatives involved: Platoon.org
Location: Seoul, South Korea
Number of containers used: 34
Gross floor area: 415 sqm
Completion: 2009
Client: Platoon.org
Type of use: exhibition center

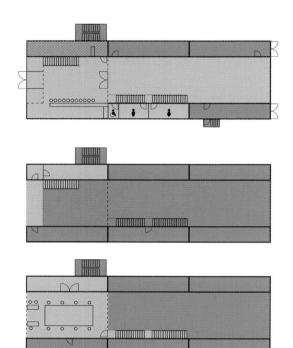

PLATOON
SEOUL, SOUTH KOREA

The PLATOON KUNSTHALLE was designed as an experimental site for artists and creatives. PLATOON KUNSTHALLE is a location where professional contemporary creativity is tested and developed. This is not a classical "white-cube" art institution. It is a creative platform for sub-culture. PLATOON Berlin opened in July, 2012. The modular architecture consists of 34 freight containers. The architecture container developed by PLATOON in collaboration with GRAFT in Seoul, Korea, won the Korean architecture prize in 2009, the RedDot award in 2010 and the design prize of the Federal Republic of Germany in 2011.

If the number of containers of todays biggest vessel were loaded onto a train it would need to be 44 miles or 71 kilometers long.

GENUSSREGAL VINOFAKTUR
VOGAU, AUSTRIA

The "GENUSSREGAL" – a commercial overall concept, that is architecture, landmark, exhibition hall and a shop in the logistics warehouse, which lends as well a new identity to the branch. The 60-meter-long, 12-meter-high set of shelves along the street is filled with overseas containers. Their inscriptions and painted logos all refer to products originating in the Steiermark. The exhibition "That's what the Steiermark tastes like" was conceptualized by BWM Architekten und Partner. Sampling the products from the region is the heart of the exhibition.

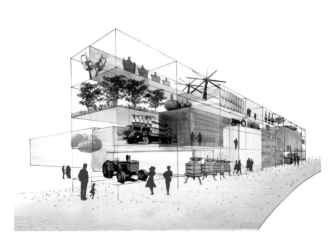

Architects: BWM Architekten
Location: An der Mur 13, Vogau, Austria
Number of containers used: 14
Gross floor area: 1,500 sqm
Completion: 2011
Client: Vinofaktur Handel GesmbH
Type of use: bistro, shop, exhibition hall

A typical ISO shipping container is made from a "weathering steel",
commonly known as "Corten steel".

GOOGLE CAMPUS
LONDON, UNITED KINGDOM

Google Campus is a seven-story co-working and event space in the center of London's Tech City, otherwise known as Silicon Roundabout. The design challenge was to take an unprepossessing seven-story office building and to create an interplay between dynamic, open, social spaces and more intimate working hubs, with flexibility to accommodate a shifting workforce and a diverse program of events. Working areas, which occupy the upper five floors of the building, are open plan. They incorporate multi-functioning container units that separate circulation from the main office space, offering hot desking, personal lockers, recycling stations, video conferencing / meeting booths and a micro kitchen.

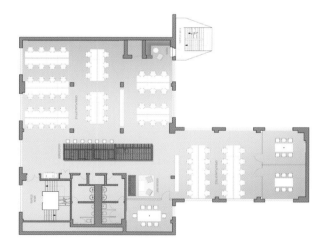

Architects: Jump Studios
Location: 4-5 Bonhill Street, London, UK
Number of containers used: 1
Gross floor area: 2,300 sqm
Completion: 2012
Client: Google
Type of use: offices

A container ship travels the equivalent of three-quarters of the way to the moon and back in one year during its regular travel across the oceans.

Roglab is a mobile creative laboratory situated in front of the old Rog bicycle factory in Ljubljana. Its main role is to promote future activities that will take place in a former factory after the revitalization of the area. The project consists of two twenty foot containers with a storage unit on top, as a part of 3D Tetris game. Inside of the pavilion there is a transformable multi-functional environment with workshop with 3D printer, cinema, gallery space or small classroom for courses with a wide span of creative fields, making this pavilion a small factory of applied education and creativity.

ROGLAB
LJUBLJANA, SLOVENIA

Architects: Arhitektura Jure Kotnik
Location: Ljubljana, Slovenia
Number of containers used: 2
Gross floor area: 29 sqm
Completion: 2011
Client: MGL and city of Ljubljana
Type of use: creative laboratory for arts and crafts

Container sizes are adjusted to the loading surface of trucks,
railroad cars or inland waterway vessels.

Architects: sculp(IT) architects
Location: Huikstraat, Antwerp, Belgium
Number of containers used: 4
Gross floor area: 60 sqm
Completion: 2007
Client: Silvia and Pieter Peerlings – Mertens
Type of use: residential

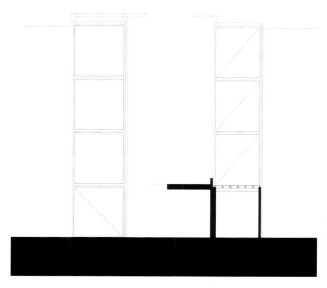

SMALLEST HOUSE OF ANTWERP
ANTWERP, BELGIUM

Four wooden floors between two existing walls, hanging in a steel skeleton, structure this house. The ground floor is for work, the first floor for dining, the second floor for relaxation, the third floor is the bedroom and the roof is for enjoying the view. The wall is made of glass. Transparency as a trump card. Where is the boundary of living if everything is visible? This transparency, where each facet of living on each floor is articulated by means of black window frameworks is like a living painting. It also knowingly refers to the former activity of prostitution in this neighborhood. The restriction of the available area, balances between need and luxury. Space is good, but also not the most important condition for good living.

Road cases are often used for storage and transport of musical instruments and materials used in theater, like props. These are specialized shipping containers.

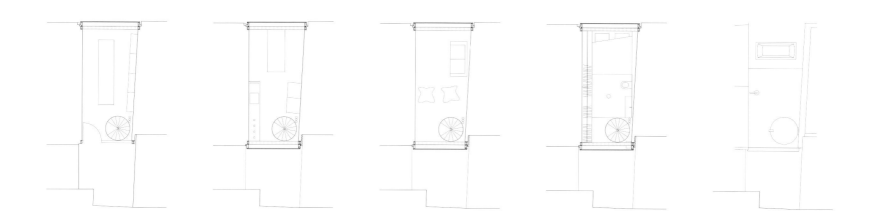

CROSSBOX
PONT PÉAN, FRANCE

In the middle of a housing estate, one house stands out: two boxes cross over each other. The surprise is the topping off with greenery and the color of the straight volumes. This project is a prototype of a three-dimensional modular and industrialized house, built with four 40 foot shipping containers. The aim is to build a low cost architect's housing with a focus on environmental issues. With industrial methods, construction time is reduced, and prices fall. Each volume presents a very simple design: living area on the ground floor, and three bedrooms on the first floor. The crossing of the two boxes provides a covered entrance and a carport.

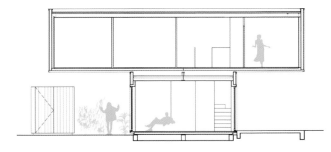

Architects: CG Architectes / 2A Design
Location: Pont Péan, Bretagne, France
Number of containers used: 4
Gross floor area: 104 sqm
Completion: 2009
Client: Clément Gillet
Type of use: residential

At least 20 million containers are currently traveling across the oceans.

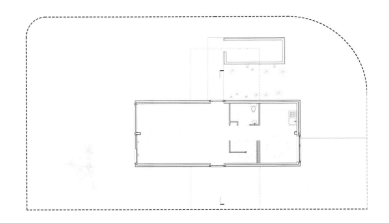
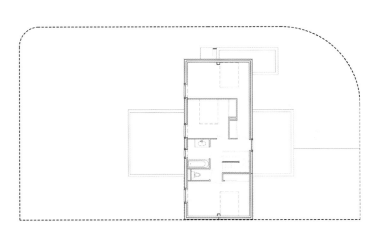

Architects: envelope A+D
Location: Hayes Street, San Francisco, United States
Number of containers used: 3
Completion: 2013
Client: Aether Apparel
Type of use: retail

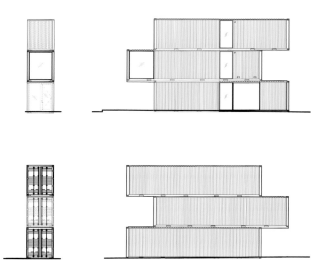

AETHER APPAREL AT PROXY
SAN FRANCISCO, USA

Aether Apparel, an online retailer that specializes in de-sign-conscious outerwear, chose the PROXY project as the site of its first stand-alone store. They were drawn to the use of shipping containers as modular units that are built to be durable rather than disposable, bold instead of drab. The three stacked containers craft an urban edge rising straight out of the asphalt. The interior space is created from the hollowing out of the lower two containers. The glass-encased cantilevered storefront window juts out over the sidewalk, drawing the gaze of pedestrians. Spanning all three floors, a custom vertical conveyor belt system makes Aether's full inventory available at the push of a button.

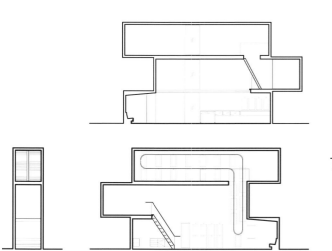

The world's first container ship was the Clifford J. Rodgers, built in Montreal in 1955.

24 shipping containers have been retrofitted and transformed into PUMA City, a transportable retail and event building that travels around the world. The building can be fully dismantled and travel using standard container networks of transportation. Originally conceived to travel on a cargo ship along with the sail boats during the 2008 Volvo Ocean Race, PUMA City has been assembled and disassembled a number of times at different international sites. The three-level container stack is shifted to create internal outdoor spaces, large overhangs and terraces. The stack is branded with the super-graphic logo of the company — fragmented as a result of the shifting.

PUMA CITY
ALL OVER THE WORLD

Architects: LOT-EK (Ada Tolla & Giuseppe Lignano)
Location: installed in China, Europe and USA
Number of containers used: 24
Gross floor area: 11,000 sqm
Completion: 2008
Client: PUMA
Type of use: retail

Each year, about 2 to 2.5 million TEUs worth of containers are manufactured.

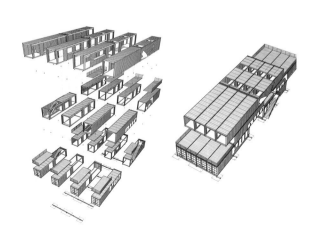
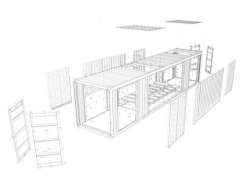
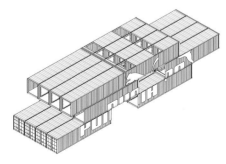

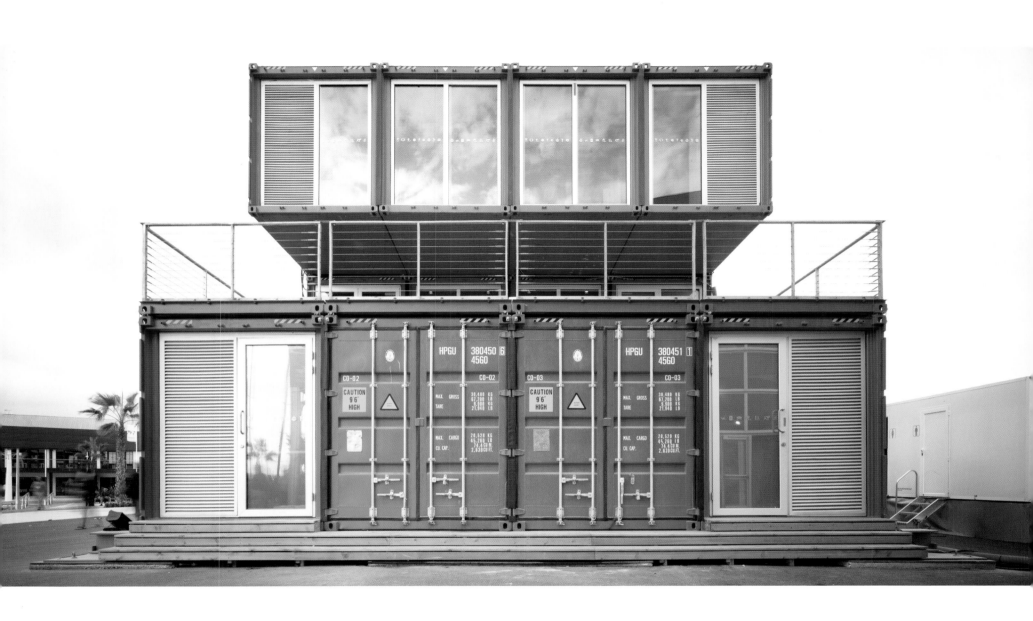

Architects: 2A Design
Location: Orgères, Bretagne, France
Number of containers used: 5
Gross floor area: 125 sqm
Completion: 2014
Client: Melle Fonlupt and M. Gillet
Type of use: residential

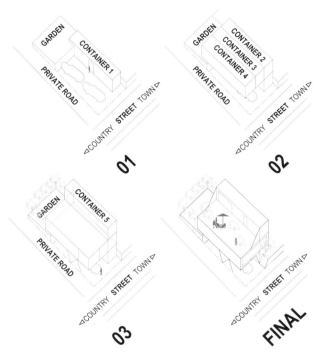

FLYING BOX
ORGÈRES, FRANCE

How can one build a multifunctional town house on a 150-square-meter plot? The main volume is lifted up from the ground floor. To observe the building code, two cars are then tucked away and integrated in the construction volume and the pedestrian entrance is covered at the same time. This volume has two faces. The first is above the street level. The house lights turn on and off with the movement of the inhabitants. The other side, on the garden, is more intimate. The first floor is oriented toward the south and overlooks a planted terrace. This space is the heart of the project. It's a place to rest and to enjoy the sun and the view. It's the best way to optimize the space at hand, by using the roof.

Architect: Christophe Nogry Architecture
Interior designer: Jean-François Godet
Location: 16 Rue Eugene Delacroix, Nantes, France
Number of containers used: 2
Gross floor area: 57 sqm
Completion: 2009
Client: Alain Lafarge
Type of use: residential

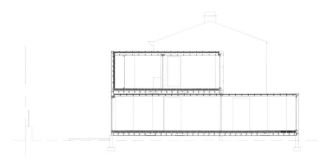

VILLA LAFARGE
NANTES, FRANCE

This project of extension is located in the city of Nantes, in front of a large residential development from the 1960s. The wish of the owner was to implant an extension on the west side of his garden, in order to enlarge the living room on the ground floor (shown), as well as adding an extra ensuite bedroom upstairs. Because of the limited width available on the plot, the idea of using maritime containers quickly appeared. The dimensions of the containers made possible to accommodate a very large collection of books, records and CDs. Jean François Godet, designer associated to the operation, drew a custom shelving unit for them.

An average ship has 200,000 individual pieces of cargo which
take around a week to load and unload.

Architects: COCHENKO (Damien Beslot, Juliette Six, Alice Leborgne), QUATORZE (Sylvain Gaufillier, Joachim Bolanos, Antoine Demarest, Romain Minod), BUTONG (Benjamin Levy, Augustin Brisedou Sagot)
Number of containers used: 1
Gross floor area: 18 sqm
Completion: 2011
Client: French Ministry of Culture / MILDT
Type of use: exhibition

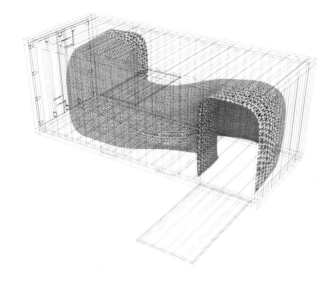

CCPP
PARIS, FRANCE

CCPP travelled to French schools in a drug awareness campaign. Through the creation of a hallucinogenic space, the visitor was given the opportunity to discuss drugs. Space, light and sound interacted with the visitor in a personal experience. Hidden triggers activate different scenes manipulating the subjects experience and creating reflections on drug use and abuse. The installation contains three continuously linked spaces – pleasure, repetition and awakening. There are no pamphlets or brochures in the installation, only a mind-opening experience and a chance to reach people visiting the installation. A chance to talk to people intrigued by architecture.

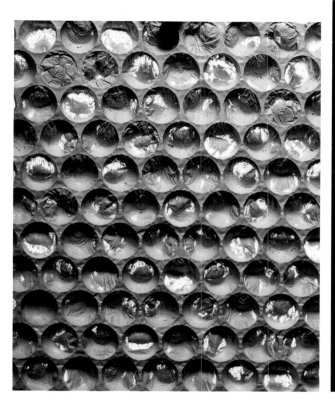

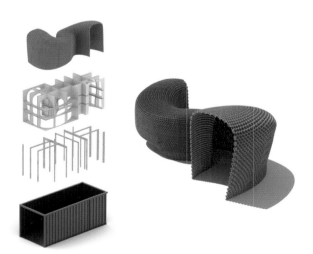

"A ship in the harbor is safe, but that's not what ships are built for." —
John Augustus Shedd, American author and professor

JIKE IDEA
BEIJING, CHINA

"Jike Idea", a 20 foot used container, is the first container garage built by Beijing Jikerzhicheng Product Design Consulting. The concept originates from Lvshe's theme activity of "dragging the box to travel" in 2012. After it is finished, the container along with designers travelled 6,000 kilometer from Beijing to Jiuzhaigou. On this trip, "Jike Idea" acted as a touring car, ministate, movie theater and fulfilled many other leisure functions. Jike Idea's nickname is "No Way". The container without a door steps over the line between indoor room and outdoor room. The space it contains can stretch out seamlessly with the environment. Its designers enjoy the process of solving problems.

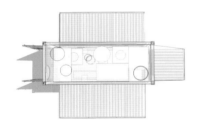

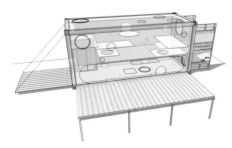

Architect: Beijing Jikerzhicheng Product Design Consulting
Design director: Keli Mo
Designers: Xianjun Yang, Zeyangping Zhang, Shixun Feng
Location: Beijin, China
Number of containers used: 1
Gross floor area: 15 sqm
Completion: 2012
Type of use: container garage for travel

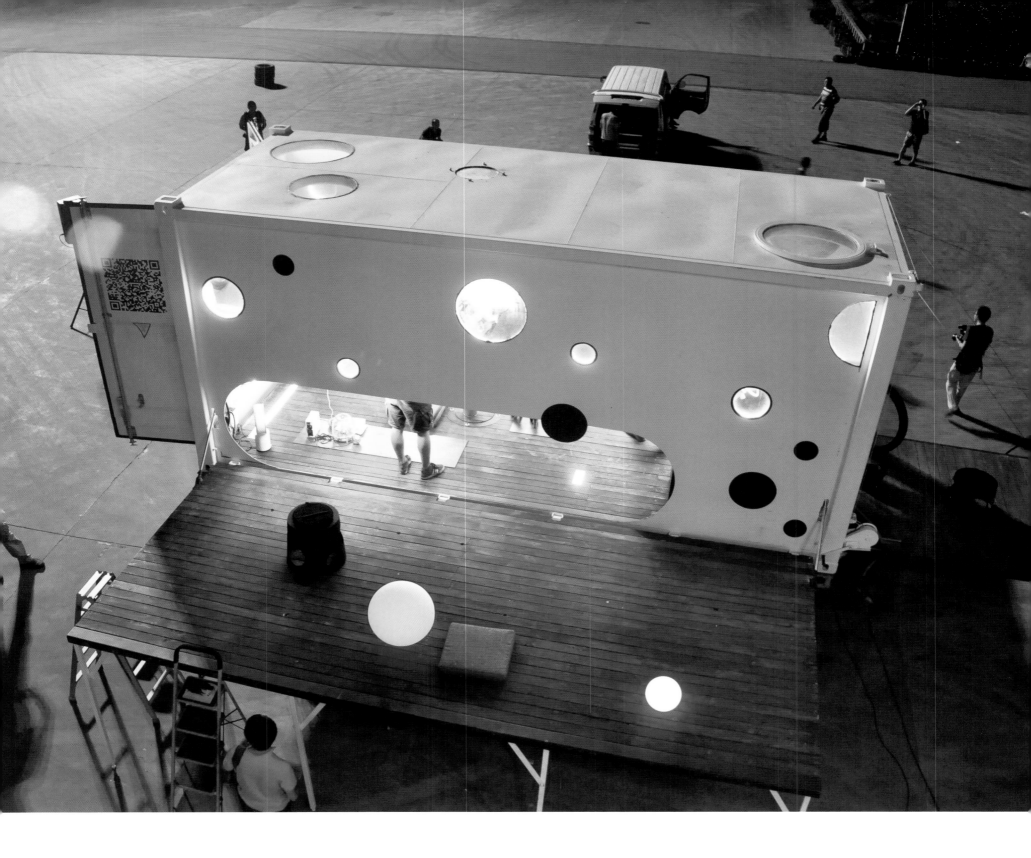

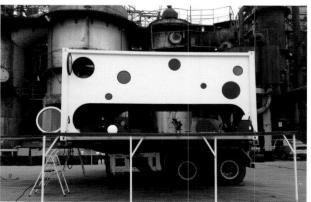

Moving an empty container is almost as costly as moving a full container.

Architects: LOT-EK (Ada Tolla & Giuseppe Lignano)
Location: Anyang, South Korea
Number of containers used: 10
Gross floor area: 2,600 sqm
Completion: 2010
Client: Kyong Park, City of Anyang
Type of use: art school

APAP
OPENSCHOOL
ANYANG, SOUTH KOREA

A shipping container structure is conceived as an open site for the OpenSchool and positioned along the river edge to activate the recreational space of the riverfront and to allow its users to be visitors, spectators and actors during the course of the public art program of APAP2010. Eight shipping containers are skewed to a 45 degree angle and combined in a fishbone pattern, generating a large arrow-like volume that hovers three meters over the landscape. The structure is strategically placed over Hakwoon park pedestrian walkway at the city level right on the edge of the drop to the river bank. The area has become a focal point for meeting, resting and the view.

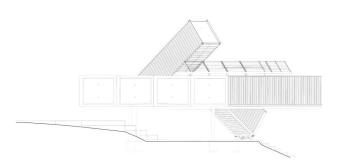

China accounts for more than 90% of the global production of containers.

Germany's largest floating building is currently docked in the Müggenburg customs port on the Veddel: the IBA DOCK. Entrance on the top floor is via a bridge. A diversified exhibition space on three floors, connected with air-spaces, a lecture area, cafeteria and an outside terrace, awaits the visitors. The office section is attached to the eastern part of the building. The three-story superstructure is mounted on concrete pontoons and modularly assembled on-site in a light-weight design with steel frames. They can be disassembled in the case of building maintenances or a change of location on the water involving passage beneath low bridges. All the modules can then be reassembled and varied if desired.

IBA DOCK
HAMBURG, GERMANY

Architect: Prof. Han Slawik / architech
Projectpartner: H. Winkelmüller
Executive Planning: bof architekten
Location: Am Zollhafen 12, Hamburg, Germany
Number of containers used: 108
Gross floor area: 1,623 sqm
Completion: 2010
Client: IBA Hamburg GmbH
Type of use: exhibition space and offices

It took until 1961 for the International Standards Organisation (ISO) to finalize global standards for containers.

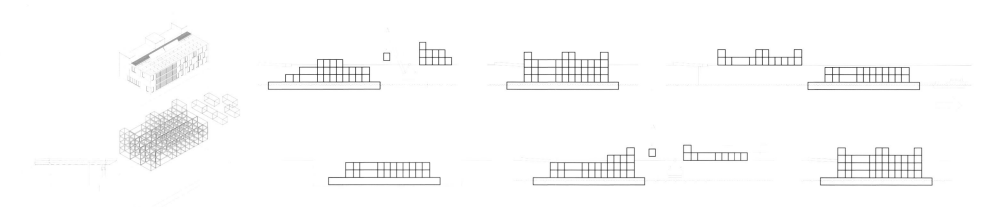

Upcycle House is an experimental project, aimed at exploiting potential carbon-emission reductions in construction through the use of recycled and upcycled building materials. In the case of Upcycle House, the reduction has been 86 % compared to the construction of a benchmark house. The loadbearing structure consists of two prefabricated shipping containers, while the roof and façade cladding is made from recycled aluminium soda-cans. Façade panels consist of recycled granulated paper, which is pressed together and heat-treated. The kitchen floor is tiled with champagne corks, and the bathroom tiles are made from recycled glass.

UPCYCLE HOUSE
NYBORG, DENMARK

Architect: Lendager Arkitekter
Design team: Anders Lendager, Christopher Carlsen, Jenny Haraldsdottir, Rune Sode, Morten Bang, Ronnie Markussen
Location: Nyborg, Denmark
Number of containers used: 2
Gross floor area: 129 sqm
Completion: 2013
Client: Realdania Byg
Type of use: residential

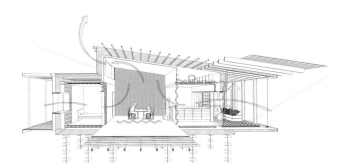

1 knot equals one nautical mile /h = 1,852 km/h ≈ 0,51444 m/s.

CONTAINER
GUEST HOUSE
TEXAS, USA

The project is the adaptive reuse of a shipping container on a light industrial site near downtown. The client lives in a warehouse on the site. The program is a guest house for visiting artists. The steel and glass sliding door and window wall open the interior to the landscape. The rest of the space is garden storage, accessed through the original cargo doors. Emphasis was placed on sustainable strategies – foremost, recycling a "one-way" container for a new and permanent use. The materials that were added to the container are both innovative – i.e. non-domestic – and appropriate to its industrial origin. The challenge was to blend these additions seamlessly with the existing shell to create a stylish and comfortable place to stay a few days, all on a modest budget.

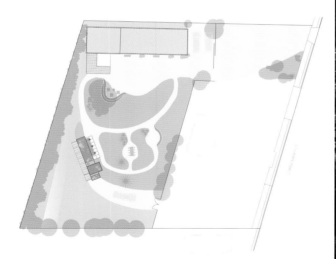

Architects: POTEET ARCHITECTS
Location: San Antonio, Texas, USA
Number of containers used: 1
Gross floor area: 30 sqm
Completion: 2010
Client: Stacey Hill
Type of use: residential

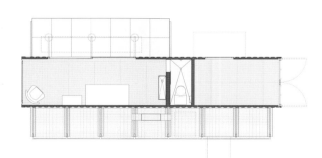

Between 1982 and 2005 containerised cargo trade grew three and a half times faster than world GDP and 40% faster than international trade overall.

INFINISKI
MANIFESTO HOUSE
CURACAVÍ, CHILE

The Manifesto house represents the Infiniski concept and its potential: bioclimatic design, recycled, reused materials, non-polluting construction systems and integration of renewable energy. The house, 160 square meters, is divided in two levels and uses three recycled maritime containers as a structure which in the form of a bridge creates an extra space inside the containers. As a consequence, with only 90 square meters, the project generates a total space of 160 square meters, maximizing and reducing the use of extra building materials. As if it had a second skin, the house 'dresses' and 'undresses' itself, thanks to ventilated external solar covers on the walls and roof. Both exterior and interior use up to 85 % of recycled, reused and eco-friendly materials, achieving a 70 % autonomy.

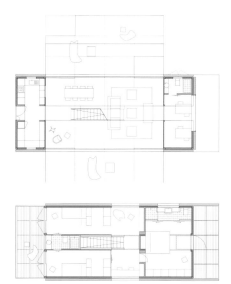

Architects: James & Mau
General contractor and manager: Infiniski
Location: Curacaví, Chile
Number of containers used: 3
Gross floor area: 160 sqm
Completion: 2009
Type of use: residential

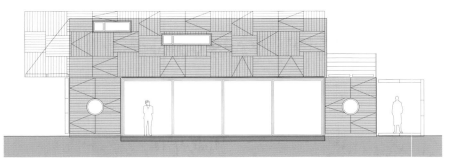
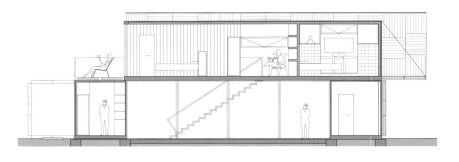
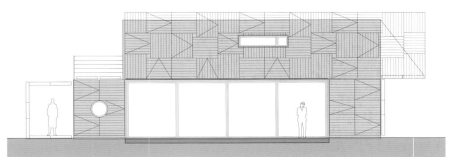
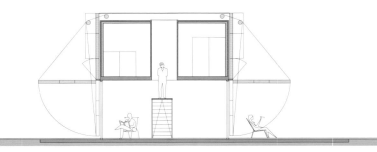

The typical cost of transporting a 20-foot container from Asia to Europe carrying over 20 tons of cargo is about the same as the economy airfare for a single passenger on the same journey.

Architects: Tongheshanzhi Landscape Design
Other creatives involved: Jiang Bo, Mo Keli, Sun Jie
Location: Changzhi City, Shanxi, China
Number of containers used: 35
Gross floor area: 5,000 sqm
Completion: 2007
Client: FMTX
Type of use: hotel

XIANGXIANGXIANG
CONTAINER HOTEL
CHANGZHI CITY, CHINA

The Xiangxiangxiang boutique container hotel is the very first boutique hotel made in China from containers. The functional space is composed from 35 containers. They are used for a courtyard, independent suite, lobby, Shixiangzhai restaurant, and a Pinxiangtang and Xunxiangjing landscape. The remarkable container look, the comfortable Chinese interior and furniture, incense and related ornamental feature, the scenery between the courtyard and Tianxia Duchenghuang all contribute to the special experience of the hotel.

As of 2010, Shanghai was the busiest container port in the world, 29,069,000 containers passed through the port annually.

Architects: Spacesmith & Davis Brody Bond
Location: Brooklyn, New York, USA
Number of containers used: 6
Gross floor area: 1,115 sqm
Completion: 2007
Client: Brooklyn Bridge Park
Type of use: recreation

BROOKLYN BRIDGE POP-UP POOL
NEW YORK, USA

Spacesmith and its partner firm Davis Brody Bond were enlisted by the Brooklyn Bridge Park to design their Pop Up Pool, a temporary swimming facility near the greenway of Brooklyn Heights' Pier 2. The site offers panoramic views of the Manhattan skyline across the river. Several tons of white sand was brought in, local saw grass was planted, and with the addition of lounge chairs and colorful umbrellas, a beach was created in Brooklyn. A welcome refuge from the summer heat and a gathering place for the local community to relax, the Brooklyn Bridge Pop-Up Pool is proof that the simplest of materials can liven up any space.

"So far no man of significance has spent his entire life on land." —
Herman Melville, American novelist

D.O.C.K.
BERLIN, GERMANY

In the fall of 2011, the Bread & Butter GmbH fair operator commissioned the planning and implementation of a container building which can accommodate twelve exhibitors of innovative fashion labels. The container building should upgrade the fair landscape.

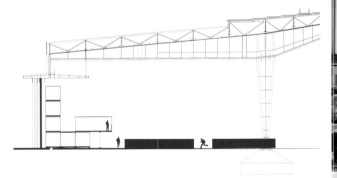

Architects: Artdepartment Berlin (Dipl.-Ing. Peter Weber)
Other creatives involved: Jonas Greubel and David O'Connell
Location: Bread & Butter, Berlin, Germany
Number of containers used: 21
Gross floor area: 400 sqm
Completion: 2011
Client: Bread & Butter
Type of use: exhibition fair stand

It is estimated that there were more than 530 million containers in the world in 2010.

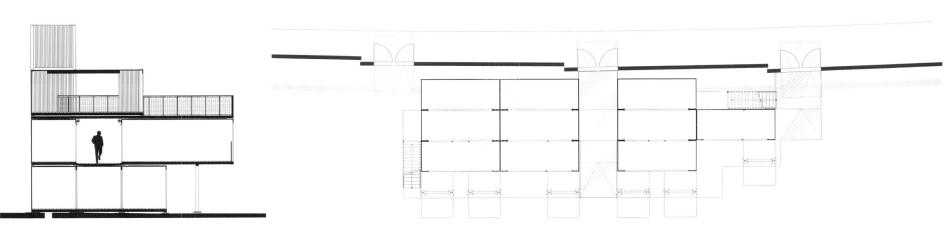

Architects: Arhitektura Jure Kotnik
Location: Trebnje, Slovenia
Number of containers used: 2
Gross floor area: 29 sqm
Completion: 2008
Client: Trimo d.d.
Type of use: residential

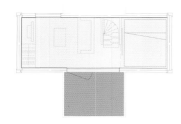

2+ WEEKEND HOUSE
TREBNJE, SLOVENIA

The 2+ is a two-level mini housing unit composed of two containers perpendicular to each other. It shows that a minimal number of containers combined in an innovative fashion offers fresh yet functional architectural solutions. The upper container provides a projecting roof above the entrance and serves to shelter the back terrace. The ceiling of the bottom container is also a terrace of the first floor. The pink – dotted façade illustrates the wide range of possibilities for tailor – made exteriors, the choice of which is as simple as deciding which mobile phone cover to put on.

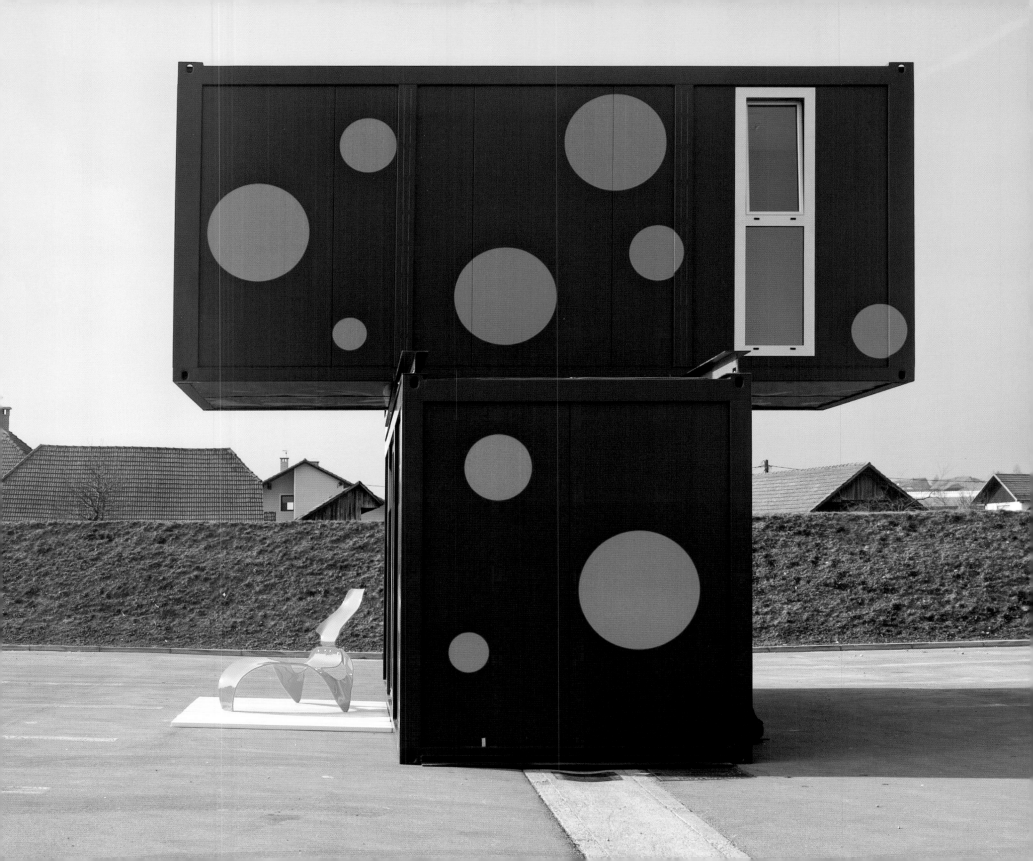

Heimstaden Office & Service Center is located in Malmö, Sweden. After the renovation the aim was to achieve a balance with their tenants, janitorial and office staff to operate in the new environment. Concrete and steel are boldly mixed with exciting materials and playful decoration. By not using traditional suspended ceilings a previously unused space could be created. To achieve a good acoustic environment, circular acoustic absorbers were suspended from the ceiling. The kitchen, built in a red modified 20-foot container is heart of the office, a natural meeting point with a mixture of modern chic and unexpected industrial feeling.

HEIMSTADEN OFFICE & SERVICE CENTER
MALMÖ, SWEDEN

Architect: Tony Rydberg / Ideas
Location: Södra Skolgatan 39, Malmö, Sweden
Number of containers used: 1
Gross floor area: 578 sqm
Completion: 2013
Client: Heimstaden
Type of use: office, service center

In addition to Spain and Portugal, China was a colossus on the high seas in the 15th century. The Chinese junks had up to nine masts and were up to 120 meters long. The famous navigator Zheng He commanded up to 30,000 crew members.

ContainR is a hybrid street installation at the nexus of video, public art, and urban design. Sited at the downtown public library courtyard, ContainR also sits at the crossroads of mountain and urban culture. Its art and sport cinema embraces public art and sustainable design. Presented by pringboard in partnership with the 2009 Vancouver Cultural Olympiad, and the 2010 Winter Games in Vancouver, ContainR showcases the best in Canadian and international sport and dance films in a mobile theater. Housed in reconditioned shipping containers with integrated alternative energy sources, the installation references Vancouver's rich history as a major port as well its role as a center for green design.

CONTAINR
VANCOUVER, CANADA

Architect: Robert Duke
Designers and project managers: Keith Doyle & Iain Sinclair
Media artist: Evann Siebens
Choreographer and producer: Nicole Mion
Location: Vancouver, Canada, and Calgary, Alberta, Canada
Number of containers used: 2
Gross floor area: 38 sqm
Completion: 2009
Type of use: exhibition

Intermediate bulk shipping container (IBC) is another container type used for shipping goods. These containers are intended for storage and shipping of fluid and bulk materials.

The Wahaca Southbank Experiment is a new two-story temporary restaurant installation, constructed from eight recycled shipping containers that have 'washed up' onto the outdoor terrace of the Queen Elizabeth Hall at the Southbank Centre in London. The idea behind using the shipping containers was not only to remind restaurant patrons of the working history of this part of the river, but also for more practical reasons: their limited height allowed fitting two floors into the volume of a single story space. Situated against the heavy concrete backdrop of the Queen Elizabeth Hall, each container is painted in one of four vibrant colors, ranging from deep turquoise to straw yellow, providing a bright contrast to the restaurant's grey surroundings.

WAHACA
LONDON, UNITED KINGDOM

Architects: Softroom
Location: Queen Elizabeth Hall, Southbank Centre, London, UK
Number of containers used: 8
Gross floor area: 380 sqm
Completion: 2012
Client: Wahaca Group
Type of use: restaurant

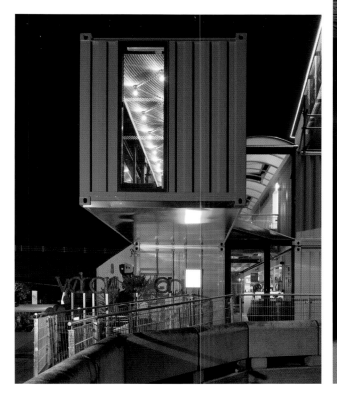

The largest container ship can carry 15,000 boxes, which would hold 746 million bananas. This would be about one banana for every person in Europe.

Thanks to his partnership with CG Architectes, B3 Ecodesign provides design for everyone. Just like choosing the color of your car, CG Architectes created the Saint Gilles project to show how you can tune up your house. It's a serial project which is finally your own, unique house. The street it shaped is unique too, due to the rhythm of the changing façades. The initial B3 Ecodesign concept was to guarantee a very high level of energetic performance too. Industrialization of the construction process permitted a drastic reduction of the building period. The turnaround time is one 100-square-meter house every four days, the completed house is ready in six weeks and you can enjoy your house after two months.

LES CHROMATIQUES
SAINT GILLES, FRANCE

Architect: CG Architectes / 2A Design
Location: Saint Gilles, Bretagne, France
Number of containers used: 57
Gross floor area: 1,064 sqm
Completion: 2011
Client: Investeam
Type of use: residential

Maersk Line is the world's largest container vessel
with a capacity of 18,000 twenty-foot containers.

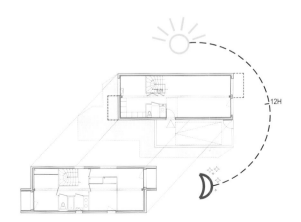

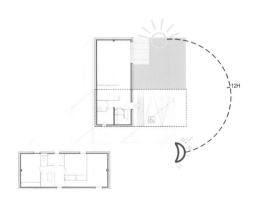

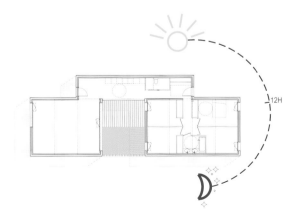

CONTAINERS
OF HOPE
SAN JOSE, COSTA RICA

The clients of the house made the very bold choice of exploring the possibility of creating a very inexpensive house made from decommissioned shipping containers. The idea was to be debt free and live the life they always dreamed of. It was important to provide them with the sunrise, the sunset, the spectacular views, while creating a feeling of comfort and home. A roof between the two containers, made from the scrap pieces of metal used to make the windows, not only creates an internal sensation of openness, but also provides cross ventilation which is good enough to keep the air conditioning turned off.

Architects: Benjamin Garcia Saxe
Location: San Jose, Costa Rica
Number of containers used: 2
Gross floor area: 100 sqm
Completion: 2011
Client: Marco Peralta and Gabriela Calvo
Type of use: residential

The client needed an art studio close to her house (which was renovated in 2008). Her requirements called for a space of about 700 square feet, a stringent budget and a simple structure that would be both inviting and reflective. The solution was to use two 40' x 8' x 9'6" shipping containers (cost: $2,500 each, delivered) perched over a 9' foundation wall / cellar. By cutting away 75 % of the floor of the containers, the architects were able to move the painting studio to a lower level via a wide staircase and take advantage of a high ceiling. The staircase itself acts as a transitional space for viewing art work. The upper floor provides a more intimate work and sitting area. The containers were painted dark charcoal to maintain continuity with the original house and to recede in the shadows of a densely wooded site.

CONTAINER STUDIO
NEW YORK, USA

Architect: Maziar Behrooz Architecture
Other creatives involved: Andrea Shapiro
Location: Amagansett, New York, USA
Number of containers used: 2
Gross floor area: 85 sqm
Completion: 2010
Client: Andrea Shapiro
Type of use: art studio

Refrigerated containers come in two categories: containers which are cooled from the on-board cooling equipment, and containers cooled with integrated cooling equipment.

Architects: Arhitektura Jure Kotnik
Other creatives involved: Gerard Noirot, Seine 13
Location: Paris, France
Number of containers used: 4
Gross floor area: 29 sqm
Completion: 2010
Client: Port of Paris
Type of use: lighthouse and promotional gallery

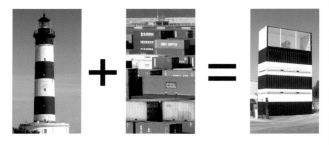

MOBILE LIGHTHOUSE
PARIS, FRANCE

The mobile lighthouse was designed to commemorate the 40th anniversary of several ports along the Seine in Paris. The idea of the design connects two basic port elements, a traditional lighthouse and containers. Lighthouses are one of most notable symbols of sea transport and can be found in all traditional ports. On the other hand, containers, as one of the main transport elements in the modern port, are also perfect to construct event architecture. Four recycled 20-foot containers form this 10-meter-high mobile pavilion. The top container has two rotating headlights, while the ground floor container hosts an information office / gallery.

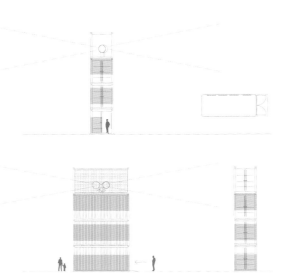

The largest ships can cost over 200 million dollars to build.

Architects: Fokkema & Partners Architecten
Location: Amsterdam, The Netherlands
Number of containers used: 8
Gross floor area: 200 sqm
Completion: 2007
Client: Municipality of Amsterdam
Type of use: town hall

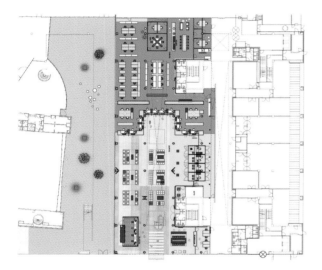

AMSTERDAM CITY HALL
AMSTERDAM, THE NETHERLANDS

The design of the Amsterdam City Hall is strikingly different from the average city council office. In collaboration with Identity Consult, Fokkema & Partners managed to create an environment that matches the current conceptions for work, as well as customer service. The choice of materials can be characterized as rough, urban and functional. An example can be found in the use of freight containers that underscore the temporary nature of the project. A more dynamic floor plan was achieved by making extra openings in existing walls. The project has become an example of how existing office buildings can be revitalized with limited budget to meet future requirements.

"Architecture is basically a container of something. I hope they will enjoy not so much the teacup, but the tea." — Yosho Taniguchi, Japanese architect

INDEX

PICTURE CREDITS

Cover front: Sergio Pirrone
Cover back (from left to right, from above to below):
Peter Lorenz, Berlin; Pedro Vannucchi; Vincent Fillon; Danny Bright; Chris Cooper

IMPRINT

The Deutsche Nationalbibliothek lists this publication in the Deutsche Nationalbibliografie; detailed bibliographic data are available in the Internet at http://dnb.dnb.de

ISBN 978-3-03768-173-2
© 2015 by Braun Publishing AG
www.braun-publishing.ch

2nd edition 2016

Editor: Sibylle Kramer
Editorial staff and layout: Maria Barrera del Amo
Translation: Geoffrey Steinherz
Graphic concept: Michaela Prinz, Berlin
Reproduction: Bild1Druck GmbH, Berlin

All of the information in this volume has been compiled to the best of the editor's knowledge. It is based on the information provided to the publisher by the architects' and designers' offices and excludes any liability. The publisher assumes no responsibility for its accuracy or completeness as well as copyright discrepancies and refers to the specified sources (architects' and designers' offices). All rights to the photographs are property of the photographer (please refer to the picture credits).